READ WITH
The Riddlers

Mossop Builds a Car

Written by Rick Vanes
Illustrated by Richard Robinson

Schofield & Sims Ltd Huddersfield England

© Schofield & Sims Ltd 1995

0 7217 0692 4

All rights reserved.
No part of this publication may be reproduced,
stored in a retrieval system, or transmitted, in any
form or by any means, electronic, mechanical,
photocopying, recording or otherwise, without
the prior permission of Schofield & Sims Ltd.

First printed 1995

Typesetting by Armitage Typo/Graphics Ltd., Huddersfield
Printed and Bound in Italy by STIGE, Turin

READ WITH
The Riddlers

Marjorie Dawe lives at Riddleton End and writes books for children. In the cottage next door lives **Mr Grimley**, who does all sorts of different jobs. But Marjorie has other neighbours as well – Riddleton End is the home of the Riddlers …

Riddlers are fairy folk who love to find out things about the world around them; they call this "Riddling". Young Riddlers are known as Tiddlers, and they spend many years having Riddling lessons from a grown-up Riddler. When they have learned enough to pass their Riddling tests, they become Riddlers themselves. There are lots of Riddlers around, but the three in these stories are:

Mossop

Mossop lives down a well in Marjorie's garden. He is the oldest Riddler and he thinks he is the cleverest. Other people are not so sure.

Tiddlup

When Tiddlup was a Tiddler, she lived with Mossop and he taught her all about Riddling. When she became a Riddler, she left the well and moved next door to live in Mr Grimley's cellar.

Middler

Middler is still a Tiddler – and a very cheeky one at that! He lives with his family in the woods and comes to Riddleton End to have Riddling lessons from Tiddlup.

One warm sunny day in spring, Mossop had an idea. "Let's get the sledge out," he said.

"But there's no snow!" said Tiddlup.

"Snow?" said Mossop.
"Who needs snow?"

"Pull, Tiddlup! Pull!" said Mossop.

But Tiddlup was not happy at all. "Why can't I ride on the sledge?" she asked.

"Because it was my idea, that's why. Now pull as hard as you can."

So Tiddlup pulled . . . and pulled . . .

and . . .

. . . she fell in the mud.

"You can't use a sledge without snow!" said Mossop. "Everybody knows that."

"Let's get some wheels and turn the sledge into a car."

"We could use these pram wheels," said Tiddlup. "But there are only two of them. To make a car, we need four wheels."

"I'll find some more wheels," said Mossop. "Leave it to me."

"Aha! Two more wheels.
Just what we need."

"We can't just take them," said Tiddlup. "That's somebody's bike."

"Rubbish," said Mossop. "Who would ride a scruffy bike like that?"

Inside the house, Marjorie was having tea with Mr Grimley.

"I've bought a bike," he said. "It's old and scruffy, but it runs well."

"Shall we go and look at it?" said Marjorie.

"You won't get very far on that!" she laughed.

"Who can have taken my wheels?" said Mr Grimley.

"I know . . .

. . . Mossop!"

"Whose idea was it to make a car?" said Mossop.
"A sledge is much safer!"

Riddling tips

Page 5   There are four different kinds of leaves in this picture. Can you spot them?

Page 6   Mossop and Tiddlup have been joined by a bird in this picture. The bird may be there whenever you turn the page from now. Will you be able to spot it? Can you see a butterfly too? He'll be flying through the pages as well.

Page 9   Can you see Mr Grimley? What do you think he is doing?

Page 10-11   There are all sorts of round shapes in these two pictures. Some are round like plates, some are round like balls, some have round holes in them. In the boxes there are also some toys of things that are used for going places. See if you can Riddle out what they are.
Can you still find the bird and the butterfly?

Page 14-15   There are three plates, three saucers and three spoons altogether in these two pictures. Can you see them?
Can you see where Mossop is? He's just outside the window! What do you think he's doing?